Keshia Starrett is a 23 year old from Derry, Ireland. She currently lives in Leeds, England, where she is creating a series of conceptual mental health poems. She has an MA Creative Writing from the University of Manchester, and a BA (Hons) English Literature from Leeds Beckett University. Her writing has appeared in various magazines and anthologies.

Hysterical

Keshia Starrett

Burning Eye

BurningEyeBooks
Never Knowingly
Mainstream

Copyright © 2017 Keshia Starrett
The author asserts the moral right under the Copyright, Designs and Patents Act 1988 to be identified as the author of this work.

All rights reserved. No part of this publication may be reproduced, stored in a retrieval system, or transmitted, in any form or by any means without the prior written consent of the author, nor be otherwise circulated in any form of binding or cover other than that in which it is published and without a similar condition being imposed on the subsequent purchaser.

This edition published by Burning Eye Books 2016

www.burningeye.co.uk
@burningeyebooks

Burning Eye Books
15 West Hill, Portishead, BS20 6LG

ISBN 978-1-911570-22-6

For my sisters who have always given everything they have for me, my mother who taught me what it means to be strong, my granny and nana, who I will miss forever, my friends who have supported me in ways I could never have imagined, and Nasser, who has backed me from the beginning.

CONTENTS

THE UNSAID THINGS	9
IT BEGINS WITH A SINGLE SELFISH CELL	12
RAPUNZEL	13
ROCK, PAPER, SCISSORS	15
MEASURING TAPES	16
BLOODY SUNDAY	18
NO SMOKING IN THE PETROL STATION	19
BUCKETS AND SPADES	20
PLEASE ALIGHT HERE FOR CONNECTING TRAINS	22
ULTRASOUND	23
THE BAKER IS INFERTILE	24
TO THE CANDLE I LIT EVERY SUNDAY	26
WINDOW-SMASHING	27
A CURRENT IS A FICKLE THING	29
DOUBTING THOMAS	30
DEATH OF THE AUTHOR	31
REASONS TO RENT INSTEAD OF BUYING	32
THE SUGAR AT THE BOTTOM OF MY TEACUP	34
THE WAKE	35
WHEN THE SWELLING GOES DOWN	36
ON A BOAT	37
MIRROR	38

THE UNSAID THINGS

I have no interest in laying blame:
a body bag at my parents' feet,
asking them to identify as I'm un-
zipped –

I can carry the autopsy out
        myself
I can carry my own
        coffin
I don't need you to tell me
        you have hope
I have hope
        in the ache of my lungs after every cigarette
I never smoked

I have never
imagined the scene
of my mother's death –
of the discovery of her body;
        her head an egg cracked
on grey tiles at the stairs' bottom

red   running
in every direction

or wrists running   like raw yolks
when a fork pokes their thin membranes

and when they ask us
were there any signs?

we will cluck
and gobble
the eggs we laid
awake thinking of
all morning –

the eggs we cannot bear
to crack
although we want them
for breakfast

I am struck by a glimpse
of genius as fleeting
as the sight of a fox's eyes
at night;
green under a torchlight
while rabbits are red
according to my uncle

I could boil the eggs
safely inside their shells

then the torch hits me
and I am caught
with the red-eyed
realisation

I'll still have to crack
                     to eat

I panic as I anticipate
which state awaits me –

the fear
     of a runny yolk
perturbing my off-red beans;

a sunset determined to split
     down the seams
and step out of line

do other families have The Troubles
for breakfast?

do they watch the sun set
every morning?

beams cracking like shallow smiles,
a cuckoo cries out from the crow's feet
around my father's eyes

I dip defiant toast-soldiers in runny yolk
and paint a single yellow line
around my mother's heart –

a warning to the cuckoo:

this is not the place   to park

IT BEGINS WITH A SINGLE SELFISH CELL

I forgot to turn the tap off and the sink over-
flowed. I couldn't seem to mop it up fast enough.
'Wasteful' was the word my mother used,
and she swore for weeks afterwards that's the reason
the crack in the tile beside the washing machine got bigger.
Like that rogue cell in your kidney that rippled all the way
into the bloodstream, a drop in the ocean – no more,
and somehow enough to upset the current and give
the moon a day off because the tide didn't take us home
afterwards.   Stranded   at sea on a lilo in the kitchen
shouting for you. And my mother cast her eyes on me
and I knew, I knew she was waiting to see a tear roll
down my cheek – another wasteful drop into the ocean,
another careless ripple, another current turned into
a whirlpool, spinning us like laundry behind the glass door,
drowning in my single, thoughtless tear.

RAPUNZEL

seventeen again;
single in a bar with				two double
anythings and seeing	double	too

more alcohol than water
and if blood is thicker
there is only interest
in a bloody mary –
however many can rescue		me
from this insatiable thirst
and the horror of mulling over
things that aren't wine

back in the days of
'eating's cheating' –
not referring to staying thin,
just wanting less
between blood and		Beefeater gin

don't interrupt this diffusion;
longing for that dazed confusion
and the sweet relief that forty-three percent
can deliver to crowded brains

the merlot stains lips
unwittingly, and the buzz is hitting
me	in a way nobody can			no more

lately I feel untouchable

I am poured
into tinted green glass;
semi-hidden and almost safe
dialling slurred voices
that might ring blue
on my brass neck

but I'm treading –
not swimming
in my hiding place

I'm in the bruised neck of wine
that's in my throat

I am a castle and merlot is my moat –
my motivation to stay afloat

I dare you now to swim across;

I'd let down my hair but can't because

I cut it
                           off

ROCK, PAPER, SCISSORS

when I was five I was convinced
my mother would never discover
the hair I cut off and hid
under a pillow, in the living room

I soon made a discovery of my own –
there wasn't much you could take
a pair of scissors to
that would remain
a secret
       for long

so last year I decided to clear the air,
aged twenty-one I got more than half my hair
chopped off for only fifteen quid
(not bad for home)

I never get a trim in Leeds,
I pull the hair from my brush
and shampoo with superglue
to avoid my ma whinging

but when I've left Derry behind
and my ma's been appeased,
I find those same scissors
before security

and walk through

whispering
              'react'

MEASURING TAPES

if the world map was a horse
you would live
thirteen hands from me
when I was nine
and now at twenty-two
you'd live six hands and time
would be measured
in fingers

but how many hands
wouldn't matter
or make sense to you
who wears a watch
with hands too small
to measure horses,

who doesn't know
I have a scar
three centimetres long
(who knows how deep),
not very neat,
glued – not stitched
below the little finger
of my left hand.

if world maps were horses
countries would be drawn,
Australia lassoed and pulled close –
not quartered
and I would not be left here
on the end of idle ropes
and a disconnected phone –
line-dancing,

hanging
my pink cowboy hat
up
on numbers no longer
recognised,

if the world map was a horse
I would not be hanging here –
a defunct cowgirl

accused of biting hands
in a deserted dance hall.

BLOODY SUNDAY

I can picture it as my mother warns me
'you're a pretty girl – make sure it doesn't get you
into trouble'

cotton bud constellations in a mascara-black night
she wiped the dirt off her face
with a pack of make-up wipes –
she wasn't allowed to shower yet

evidence evidence evidence
is a strange word when you type it
a few times
in a row

I hear they used to cleanse a woman
in chapel after she had given birth,
or was it after her period?

now we're driving past the chapel
and my aunt is blessing herself in the name of the father
and of the son
and I'm cursing while
she's praying;

absolution and erasure are not
synonyms
but old habits die hard
so I join in

Bishop Daly is dead
and I picture him waving his white handkerchief
stained red –

it isn't her blood
but it might as well be

NO SMOKING IN THE PETROL STATION

I
in the garden my granny
covered me in butter
until I was burnt to a crisp and crippled
by sunstroke – chubby arms outstretched,
swaying among the rows of roses.

if I'd been planted properly
maybe I'd have learned to rise
but my sun-shy tension was disguised
beneath the ground

II
my face burned red under the butter
preserved in the bogs of Heaney's poems,
when I saw the old man's house.
petrol bombs swaddled in outgrown pyjamas –
did we put them back or tip them out?

the burnt window blinds accuse me
as the wrinkles crack along his cheeks.
mummy said he had to throw himself
out the window,
arms outstretched
and scrambling.

are they still underneath
that pink grown-up tree
like the soil cemented
under my bitten fingernails?

did we put them back or tip them out?

BUCKETS AND SPADES

for Ciara

when you told me your hair was
'ginger', after years of 'strawberry-blonde' –
'auburn' for a brief stint

I looked at your pale face,

eyes mum-green, 'ginger' hair aglow
and I could tell you wanted
to dig a hole
like we did when we were children –

me, armed with a red spade;
you, with a face freckling, burnt
angry at the turret that can't be turnt   out
of the castle-shaped bucket
without   crumbling,

and instead of you burying me
because I was smallest
(a likely excuse),
I'll bury you and every freckle
or mole that might change
when we get old

because you're the smallest now
and you need to hide
from the 'not' that's been tied
to the end of your 'I do'.

you feel the sand –
feel the pressure as I stand on silt
covering your chest
(let's hide the signs that we've grown up –
let's hide the sewn-shut space where a breast   was)
and gasp in gaps
between   an asthma attack
and the most comfort we've felt
in months.

I stamp my feet harder
drawing a circle in the sand –
buckets and spades;
worn-red shades in worn-out hands,
surrounding you
as we watch the tide come in.

you tell me the ring must be gone –
completely erased –
before I'm allowed to
dig you up, and

call the ocean to let him know
we need salt for the merlot   stains
on the living room carpet.

PLEASE ALIGHT HERE FOR CONNECTING TRAINS

one of my favourite places to stay
in Ireland has the banshee's cry
of a train track rumbling
through my stomach every day.

now in my home away – England,
I hum along each morning
to the trains passing
and I play
house, like a child.

standing at the window
of the Belfast bedroom,
I play chicken with the faces –
hundreds at a time
the train track taking them from me
haunted by my naked post-shower body
fingers tracing the ribbed tracks
unsure which platform
to depart
from.

the same passengers
rumble past my haunt
in Leeds, I hear them but I can't see,
blind's man buff has me prepared –

I wonder do they feel me here
under this skylight of a window
in their gut?

I flash in static onto their TVs,
'the train goes running along the track,
chiggity can, chiggity can,
I wish it was mines,
I wish it was mines,'
ten years old in a school uniform
with a badly cut fringe standing on end,

stomach rumbling along, even then.

ULTRASOUND

As I crowned I saw   a slice   at the
end of her; an exit wound that can't or   won't   heal,
which is morning or night?
Can she feel   me –
a train going through
my mountain,
my mother?

As if I moved   carriage three times
to be
forward-facing on the right-hand side,
sea-side

but the tide couldn't take the salt out of my
sweat
on that hospital bed of a train.

The windows become mirrors,
too black to obscure
my face –
she never saw my face,
my mountain.

Mountains don't bleed red, you know,
they bleed dirty dishwater and sweat as their carriages are carried
away
to the drying rack.

Nobody knows   loss   like my mountain –
the tide takes everything from her and its reach
increases as the children on Downhill Beach
wave.

I look for her every time I ride the train.
I only know her name,   'Binevenagh',
but she doesn't see my face or me,

the windows are black
and I can't see   out.

THE BAKER IS INFERTILE

I'm a bun in the oven
turned off at the wall.

Derry pushes me and suddenly
I'm back
to cake mix, eggs cracked, a cup of flour
and yolks split
by a mean fork that meddles in my affairs –
mix two parts flour
to one part milk.

I didn't have the heart
to tell the baker
I'm not that sweet –
go easy on the sugar.

I'm not the maternal type –
put the milk away
(it's off).

My mother always made me
smell the milk,
I always know when it goes
because I have a nose
for these things
(and it's nothing to do
with the affair – I'd swear
on anything, even your grave).

I'm a bun in the oven
turned off at the wall.

You should've used
the self-raising flour
or a taste at least
of bicarbonate soda –
even yeast would've done
the job.

I'm a bun in the oven

that won't rise

again –
the third time isn't always
the charm.

I'm standing near the back of mass
holding a parish bulletin to prove
I was here

turned off at the wall.

TO THE CANDLE I LIT EVERY SUNDAY

we were always told not to put our fingers in our mouths.

someone should've let her know too,
she's been genuflecting
to a toilet bowl
chewing on her own fist trying to dislodge
your blood – transfigured and so
she hasn't fallen off the wagon;
she said her own prayers over you at home,
(red or rosé only)
self-anointed and justified.

the man up the road who lived on
your body and blood
fed you to the pigeons
every day at noon –
his name was Jack;

showed me to hold you
in my palms,
taught me to be the still
point in her storm;
the hurricane's eye,

I say my prayers
to weather reporters
at six o'clock each evening:

I am a lighthouse
that needs no keeper
but help me keep her
        alight

        Amen.

WINDOW-SMASHING

in a pub about to drop dead
from a vitamin d
deficiency
because the windows have been
boarded up –
                that's a lie

they've been
bricked up   because

people kept putting them in
instead of putting bottles down
was not an option
for
a girl with eyes like pints
downing rainclouds
'best price per percentage   please'

with hands too cold to hold or throw
a brick and so   sticks   stoned
staring   at
windows bricked
up crypt thick
                        to keep out other bricks

and any light that might
t r i c kle in a little
by other means than the fickle liquor
measured by fingers that know
they will visit the throat
later to retrieve a small percentage
(that's interest for you)

listen to the dull thud of bricks
aiming for a s-h-a-t-t-e-r-i-n-g
sound and instead achieving
a lowly clank or scrape;
a metal chain attached to   nothing
a key that can't quite turn in the too-small space

their disappointment is tangible
their parents must have cried
as they looked on from their solid position
poised in camaraderie
and found their youngest lying
with glassy eyes in unmade beds –
not a part of anything
screaming obscenities at
wet cement

that's her haunting ground –
building sites where she can be
the thing that binds and isn't bound

so raise your empty glass to her
in a rigor mortis manner
heave it now against the bricks
the disappointed parents and the pricks
in the name of   unmade beds
and   unbuilt walls

cackle at the sound of
s-h-a-t-t-e-r-e-d   glass

feel the blood spatters at last
cutting up hands on broken shards

there is a keen blistering sting in my nose –
I smell nettles on a hot day

this is all I know

A CURRENT IS A FICKLE THING

my ma always warned us to watch
for the tide coming in
because a current could take you out
in a minute
and she was right one Christmas Eve
(the year I was getting a trampoline) –

we weren't paying attention
to much but the presents,
waist-deep in cardboard boxes
when the current came in
and took my sister
crushing her against the wall –
tide curled tight against her throat.

I watched safe aboard
The Titonic –
my boxy ship and
sanctuary,

I should've thrown a life ring but
I was afraid the current would reel me in
like a fish conceding on a hook.

on the ever-favoured Friday night,
the latest current took her again
and I charged *The Titonic* and squashed and ripped –

they say a good captain goes down with the ship.

I say I wouldn't know
that part of the shipyard.

DOUBTING THOMAS

I try to find an angle
into you,
but the protractor never worked
for me.

I always had to use
the tracing paper trick,
rotating around a yellow HB
pencil pinned at the centre,
counting the turns –

I needed to see what was
underneath –
you're not as easy to see
through,
I can't seem to trace you

or count the turns
you took,
I've spent years examining
the margins
of my maths books.

You told me I'd have been better
at maths if you'd been here.

I plaster Factor 50 on
to my sheet-white skin and nod,
explaining that SPF
means how long it will last – not
how strong it is.

DEATH OF THE AUTHOR

a fortune-teller once had the misfortune
of greeting me with promises
of answers

so I sat, a zip-lipped cynic
eyeballing him as I held his hands
and he professed:

a writer,
two universities,
a ring – not marriage though

and as I picked my final tarot card,
turning it over
in my sweaty palm,

he took great lengths to tell me
that the reaper didn't necessarily
mean my death –

just the death of something.

at the end I was allowed
to ask one final question:

how did this begin?

it turns out his granny was a tout
and she told everyone he knew
more than he was letting on.

REASONS TO RENT INSTEAD OF BUYING

little house tattooed into my brain,
they're coming for you

little house tattooed into my brain,
I question your structural integrity

you're a result of skin caving in
under too much pressure –

the bones of your picturesque
thatched roof splint/ered
by one ungloved, unsteady hand

a tattoo gun is a reflex hammer
and I am a nail with no head

they left your beams
lobotomised –
the doctors who say
I was lucky   there were lasers
to burn you away

my mother didn't have the same luck at all,
they cut you out of her prefrontal lobe –
a mortal sin, they said
when she slid to the hospital

she'd been wearing jumpers all summer
to hide her mistake,
a stick-'n'-poke with dirty ink,
heavy sleeves/
              sweaty wrists

you can be sure any house I own
will be modern
will be slick as wrists
and the ceiling
will be inundated with elaborate chandeliers

don't take this personally
but my therapist made me compile
a list of your faults:

thin mouldy walls, creaky doors, cupboards won't close
tight, holes in the curtains letting in light
but worst of all
the smell of bread in the toaster
that never pops up
'til it's charred

'til I stick a knife in and forget
to turn the plug off at the wall

little house tattooed into my brain,
I know you didn't mean any harm
and before the days of fire alarms

I would have afforded you the kindness
of a quiet match
lit in the night

THE SUGAR AT THE BOTTOM OF MY TEACUP

In the soft creak of a morning
the kettle is my only friend
and I encourage it to whistle –
to stir the sugar in my brain;
to rot my teeth.

I whisper back –
I have not forgotten
the tea bag stewing in the cupboard
hidden in a baby-blue fine chipped
china teapot,
immersed in cold boiled water;

the teabag that refuses
to diffuse and colour any water
unlike the blues that won't relent
in consuming your skin
as I sit with you;

the teabag that refuses
to diffuse and colour any water
unless it's in my favourite cup –
a tacky orange one that reads
'smart ass'; a gift from you.

In the soft creak of a morning
I drink black tea
and cover the mirrors;

I whisper back
with no one to wake

but you.

THE WAKE

to you, mummified in the Manchester Museum

did you know an elastic band
is enough to keep
your razor mouth shut?

bandaged up as if
they want to keep you safe;
as if they care, as if
you had a sore jaw and they
needed, or wanted,
to let you heal.

you appeal to me,
swaddled menace
in muddied bandages –
you need your rest
before the stitches
come out.

morbid creatures we are,
demanding an open casket
to mourn you,
who looks as if
you want
to open your jaws
one last time

and bite down
hard.

WHEN THE SWELLING GOES DOWN

for Annie Starrett

Dear   ,

I didn't write the letter in pencil
with an eraser by my side.
There was no address on the envelope –
a stamp I couldn't afford licked
and I hoped it would stick
when I erased your name.

I didn't tell you that I still climb that massive hill
to your house and stand outside
where we buried you that Friday –
my eyes always wide when I try to take in
the buildings stretching on for miles,
and I never lose sight of the three houses
that appear to spell out 999
on the other side of the river
(ribs attached to this town's spine).

It wasn't a view to die for but God knows
it is beautiful.

I used to wonder where the lights
from the Halloween fireworks went
but now I know –

they're yours and mine, our dotted homes,
a luminous web from a bird's-eye view –
purple gone blue when the lights trickle
out of the night; when the swelling goes down
and the bruise
        fades.

I couldn't look away then

and I can't now.

I didn't open the envelope when it came through
the letter box –
addressed:
        return to sender.

ON A BOAT

Barcelona
        pretty little concrete city
on the sea

surfing champion
        two years running
faster than veins –
        even arteries

someone pin-pricked my Barcelona;

all hell has broken
        loose

my heart is palpitating in my throat

Gaudi's house looks
        straight to me

Barcelona
        pretty little concrete city
surfing oceans
        bleeding out
in ambulances

sirens are calling out from streets where
        strange men offer me MD

I can't be here with you
        Barcelona

I'm putting ear plugs in
        to drown out waves and skin
                                  breaking

finding needles in haystacks is easier
        than arms

when you're this   far   gone

MIRROR

for Julia Gallagher

someone switched off her
reflection.

the family asked to keep it
anyway
but it reveals
nothing.

a faceless lady with a blue bonnet
decorates the mirror and attempts to stare
out

waiting for her
return.

                                        frozen by a
                                        child's
                                        stare

until a birthday candle blew it   back onto
                                                      the wall

and she appeared
at last.

one eye blue and
one eye black

revolving in its socket

                      now stared back granny-smith-green

                      and she smiled at me.

                      I panicked, noticing the switch.

ACKNOWLEDGEMENTS

Versions of 'Buckets and Spades', 'Window-Smashing' and 'Reasons to Rent Instead of Buying' first appeared in *The Honest Ulsterman*. 'It Begins with a Single Selfish Cell' first appeared in *Ink, Sweat & Tears*. 'Ultrasound' first appeared in *The Best Poetry Book in the World* (edited by Jenn Hart and Clive Birnie, 2017, Burning Eye). Versions of other poems here formed part of my Master's dissertation at the University of Manchester.

Thanks to the very talented Carmen Horner for the artwork, and to the equally talented Aimee Harkin for the digital editing.

www.ingramcontent.com/pod-product-compliance
Lightning Source LLC
LaVergne TN
LVHW041559070426
835507LV00011B/1185